Y0-CJE-830

Date: 11/27/19

J 531.6 HAR
Harrison, Paul,
Fabulous forces /

PALM BEACH COUNTY
LIBRARY SYSTEM
3650 SUMMIT BLVD.
WEST PALM BEACH, FL 33406

Zac Newton Investigates

Fabulous Forces

WORLD BOOK

www.worldbook.com

World Book, Inc.
180 North LaSalle Street
Suite 900
Chicago, Illinois 60601
USA

For information about other World Book publications, visit our website at www.worldbook.com or call 1-800-WORLDBK (967-5325).

For information about sales to schools and libraries, call 1-800-975-3250 (United States), or 1-800-837-5365 (Canada).

© 2018 (print and e-book) by World Book, Inc. All rights reserved. No part of this publication may be reproduced, stored in a retrieval system, or transmitted in any form or by any means (electronic, mechanical, photocopying, recording, or otherwise) without written permission from World Book, Inc.

WORLD BOOK and the GLOBE DEVICE are registered trademarks or trademarks of World Book, Inc.

Library of Congress Cataloging-in-Publication Data for this volume has been applied for.

This edition: ISBN: 978-0-7166-4057-8 (hc.)
ISBN: 978-0-7166-4056-1 (set, hc.)

Also available as: ISBN: 978-0-7166-4063-9 (e-book)

Printed in China by Shenzhen Wing King Tong Paper Products Co., Ltd., Shenzhen, Guangdong
1st printing July 2018

Produced for World Book by White-Thomson Publishing Ltd
www.wtpub.co.uk

Author: Paul Harrison
Editor: Izzi Howell
Design/Art director: Claire Gaukrodger
Illustrator: Rob Davis/The Art Agency

Cover artwork: © Doug Holgate

Batman is a registered trademark of DC Comics, New York City, New York, USA.

Frisbee is a registered trademark of Wham-O, Inc., Emeryville, California, USA.

Iron Man is a registered trademark of Marvel Worldwide Inc., New York City, New York, USA.

Star Wars, Darth Vader, the Force, and Lightsaber are registered trademarks of Lucasfilm, Ltd, San Francisco, California, USA.

Staff

Executive Committee

President
Jim O'Rourke

Vice President and
Editor in Chief
Paul A. Kobasa

Vice President, Finance
Donald D. Keller

Vice President, Marketing
Jean Lin

Vice President, International Sales
Maksim Rutenberg

Vice President, Technology
Jason Dole

Director, Human Resources
Bev Ecker

Editorial

Director, New Print
Tom Evans

Managing Editor
Jeff De La Rosa

Librarian
S. Thomas Richardson

Manager, Contracts & Compliance
(Rights & Permissions)
Loranne K. Shields

Manager, Indexing Services
David Pofelski

Digital

Director, Digital Product Development
Erika Meller

Manager, Digital Products
Jonathan Wills

Graphics and Design

Senior Art Director
Tom Evans

Senior Web Designer/Digital Media Developer
Matt Carrington

Manufacturing/Production

Manufacturing Manager
Anne Fritzinger

Proofreader
Nathalie Strassheim

A glossary of terms appears on p. 94.

Contents

- **6**   Chapter 1: A Race Against Time
- **13**   Chapter 2: A Different Kind of Hero
- **21**   Chapter 3: Rolling Stones
- **30**   Chapter 4: The Wright Idea
- **41**   Chapter 5: Faster, Higher, Stronger
- **50**   Chapter 6: A Little Leverage
- **58**   Chapter 7: Under Pressure
- **65**   Chapter 8: Look Out Below!
- **74**   Chapter 9: The Secret Weapon
- **82**   Chapter 10: Give Me a Break
- **92**   Meet the Scientists
- **94**   Glossary
- **95**   Additional Resources
- **96**   Index

Zac Newton and friends

Zac

Zac is a junior genius and inventor of the Backspace app. The app allows Zac and his friends to take virtual trips through time and space, just by snapping a selfie.

Lucía

Lucía has a sharp mind and an even sharper wit. She pretends to be too cool for school, but inside she burns to learn about science.

Marcus

Quick-thinking Marcus is always ready with a joke. Although he loves to clown around, he knows more than he lets on.

Ning

Ning likes to run, jump, and play ball. She may be the youngest of the group, but nobody's going to push her around.

Orbit

Zac's dog, Orbit, loves to join Zac and his friends on their adventures. He's not afraid of anything—except loud noises.

Chapter 1
A Race Against Time

The Frisbee seemed to hang in the air for a second. Then the dog jumped and snapped his mouth shut on it in one easy move.

"Nice catch, Orbit," called Lucía.

Zac Newton looked up from the driveway, where he was sorting through old bicycle parts. He smiled.

"Are you sure you won't join us?" Lucía asked.

"Thanks, but I'd rather get started on this," Zac replied. "I'm sure I can put together a bike from all these bits and pieces. There's a pretty good chain and pedals, and the wheels are mostly okay. This frame's a little rusty, but it seems sturdy enough… I think I can do it. If you want to help, you can start scraping off some of this rust."

"Well, good luck with that, but playing with Orbit sounds more fun," said Ning. "Okay, Orbit, it's my turn. Ready to see some real skills?"

Ning flung the Frisbee. It swooped through the air, nearly skimming the top of Zac's head.

"Hey!" he shouted.

"Perfect throw," giggled Ning.

The Frisbee soared just out of Orbit's reach, rising on a stiff breeze. It came to rest in the branches of the big oak tree in Zac's front yard. Orbit looked up eagerly, waiting for the Frisbee to drop. But the only thing that came down was a shower of leaves.

"Uh-oh," said Ning.

"Great shot, Ning!" said Lucía sarcastically.

"Do you have a ladder, Zac?" Ning asked.

Zac put down the bent bicycle wheel he was holding. He looked up to where the Frisbee was stuck.

"Hmm… I doubt I have a ladder long enough to reach that," said Zac.

"And I'm not sure climbing a ladder that high is such a great idea, anyway," said Lucía. "Well, that's the end of that, then. Nice work, Ning."

"It wasn't my fault," Ning protested. "The wind caught it!"

"She's got a point," said Zac. "It's pretty windy today."

Marcus rolled up on his skateboard. With an expert

kick, he flipped the skateboard into his hand.

"Hey, have you all seen this?" Marcus asked. He held up a piece of paper. Zac took it from him.

"It's a flier, an advertisement for a cart race." Zac read it out loud. "Open to all ages. Any design, but no engines."

"Sounds great," said Ning. "I'm in. When is it?"

"Hmm… tomorrow," Zac replied.

"Wow, that doesn't give us much time," said Lucía. "Do you think we can come up with a racing cart by then?"

"Oh, that's plenty of time," Zac replied.

"You always say that," said Lucía, suspicious.

"No, really," said Zac. "We can build one. We probably already have the materials we need. I've got all kinds of stuff in the garage."

Marcus peered into the cluttered garage. "You mean you've got all sorts of junk!"

"Junk!" Zac yelped. "I'll have you know that everything in that garage is a valuable scientific resource!"

"Yeah, like I said, junk!" teased Marcus.

Zac smiled. "Seriously, though, I've never built a racing cart before. Have any of you?"

The other three children shook their heads.

"The closest I've come was a little red wagon I used to have," said Ning. "My dad used to pull me around the park in it when I was little. I loved it. That's where I developed my need for speed!"

"Well, I'm sure we can figure out how to make a winning racing cart," said Zac. "It's really just a matter of forces," he mumbled, thinking out loud.

"Forces? You mean like in Star Wars?" joked Marcus. "I'm Darth Vader, and I will use the Force to win the cart race for the Dark Side." He jumped around pretending to swing a lightsaber.

"Sssccchhhhhhuuuummm, vvvvvvvvvvvuuummmm!"

"Not like that," sighed Zac. "Ning was talking about her dad pulling her around in the wagon. There were lots of different forces at work there. Her dad was creating forces when he moved, not to mention the pulling of the cart, the resistance of friction between the wheels and the ground, and … No, hold on a minute. I'm making this sound really boring."

"Yeah, come on, Zac," said Lucía, pulling an apple from her backpack. "You usually explain things way better than that."

"Thank you. And that," said Zac, grabbing the apple, "gives me an idea. I know someone who can help here." He pulled his cell phone from his pocket. "Gather around, everyone. There's someone I'd like you to meet."

Chapter 2
A Different Kind of Hero

"Now this is more interesting than listening to you babble, Zac," said Marcus. He smiled as the friends crowded together.

"Through the miracle of my greatest invention, the Backspace app," Zac announced, waving his cell phone, "we can visit any time in history."

"We know. We know," said Lucía, rolling her eyes.

"All we have to do is gather in for a selfie," Zac continued. He held the phone at arm's length. "Can you all see yourselves on the screen?" he asked.

"Push the button, already," Ning cried impatiently.

Zac checked one last time that he could see all their faces. Then he tapped the screen.

FLASH!

ZUMMMMMMmmmmmmm...

There was a bright light, and suddenly everything changed. Zac's yard and driveway disappeared. The friends were now completely surrounded by a virtual world. Where Zac's oak tree had been, there stood an apple tree heavy with fruit. Beneath it, a man sat in the shade writing on a piece of paper. The pen he held looked to be made from a feather. He wore a long coat with large cuffs. On his head sat a long, white wig.

"Who's that?" asked Lucía.

"That is Sir Isaac Newton," answered Zac, beaming with pride. "He's the man I'm named after. He's one of my family's scientific heroes, and this is Lincolnshire, in England."

"They sure dress funny in England," said Marcus.

Zac gave him a stern look.

"I'm joking," said Marcus. "I know this is a big deal for you. How long ago was this?"

"The year is 1665," Zac explained. "We're on the grounds of Sir Isaac's boyhood home. He was supposed to be studying at Cambridge University, but he had to leave because of the plague. The plague is a deadly disease that was sweeping across Europe at the time. Many people fled to the country, to escape the spread of the plague. In a weird way, that worked out pretty well for Sir Isaac, because it was here that he made a scientific breakthrough."

The children watched as an apple fell from the tree. It bounced on the ground near Sir Isaac.

"And there we go," said Zac proudly, "his big discovery!"

"What? That was it? Nearly getting hit on the head by a piece of fruit? What did he discover—that it's dangerous to sit under apple trees?" said Marcus in disbelief. "Your family has some weird heroes, Zac. I should show you some Batman comics sometime. Now that's what I call a hero."

"That's not it at all," laughed Zac. "The apple made him wonder why things fall down, rather than up, or why they don't just float in the air. Sir Isaac realized that something was pulling the apple down. And that thing was gravity."

"So I'm guessing gravity is a kind of force," said Lucía.

"That's right!" Zac replied. "A force is basically a push or a pull. Forces change the way an object moves—the object's motion. Good old Sir Isaac here came up with three scientific laws called the laws of motion."

"So, he's like the movement police," said Ning with a smile.

"No, a scientific law isn't like a law that tells people how to behave," Zac explained. "A scientific law just describes how something works."

"Cool, but unless that guy rescued someone from an evil mega-villain, he's still not a hero in my book," said Marcus. "I don't care how many laws he made up."

"What if his laws of motion can help us to win the race?" asked Zac.

"In that case, I'll make an exception. Just this once, though," said Marcus.

Zac tapped the screen of his phone, and the virtual world around them disappeared. The friends were back in Zac's yard.

"That always makes me kind of dizzy," said Ning.

"Okay," said Lucía, "how do we get this racing cart started? I've never seen a cart being pulled in a race before. If anything, I've seen one being pushed."

"Absolutely right," Zac replied. "Like I said before, forces are basically pushes and pulls. It's better to push a racing cart than to pull it for one excellent reason—you won't get run over if you fall."

"Yeah, that would certainly ruin our chances of winning," laughed Marcus.

"But there's an even bigger threat to our chances," said Zac. "It's called friction."

"Friction? What's that?" asked Lucía.

Zac started to explain. "It's pretty straightforward. Friction is a property that makes objects in contact res—"

"Use the phone! Use the phone!" chanted Ning and Marcus.

"Oh, all right," said Zac. "Come on, you know the drill."

The friends gathered together as Zac opened up the Backspace app and punched in some numbers.

"Lucía, why do you always make kissy faces at the camera?" asked Marcus. "You do realize it isn't taking an actual picture?"

Lucía jabbed an elbow into Marcus's ribs, sending the ticklish boy sprawling out onto the lawn.

FLASH!

ZUMMMMMmmmmmmm...

Zac's yard disappeared as the friends returned to the virtual world.

"Where's Marcus?" asked Ning, as a scene began to appear around them.

"He must not have been in the camera frame when I set off the app," said Zac. "He can see us, but he can't see what we see."

"Serves him right," said Lucía."

"Actually, never mind where Marcus is," said Ning. "Where are we?"

Chapter 3
Rolling Stones

The familiar surroundings of Zac's yard had been replaced by rolling green hills. There was not a road or a building in sight. But, there were groups of men dressed in simple clothing made from animal skins. Some were digging in the ground using tools made from animal horn. Others were dragging a huge block of stone past Ning, Lucía, and Zac.

The block rolled along on a track of logs laid side by side. As the block passed a log, workers grabbed that log and moved it to the front of the line. The rumbling of the heavy block shook the ground under their feet.

"We're back in England," said Zac, "at a place called Stonehenge, to be precise, about 4,000 years ago."

"What are these guys doing?" asked Lucía. She watched as the men dragged the block toward a half circle of upright stones.

"They're building a stone circle," Zac replied.

"Why?" asked Ning. "That sounds like a lot of work."

"Well, no one is entirely sure. Many historians think that Stonehenge was used for rituals of some sort, but exactly how it all worked is still a mystery. The people who made it didn't write anything down," said Zac.

"So why are we here?" asked Lucía. "What do stone circles and rituals have to do with a racing cart?"

"It's not what they're building, but how they're building it," said Zac. "I thought this would be an ideal place to demonstrate friction." He pointed at a small stone block sitting on the ground nearby. "Give that block a push."

Lucía and Ning heaved and puffed, but they could not get the block to budge.

"It's way too heavy!" Ning complained.

"I'm not surprised. You see, when you try to slide the rock along the ground, the rock and the ground resist being moved against each other. This is what we call friction," Zac explained. "Now give that other block a push." He pointed at a larger block sitting on some rollers nearby.

"If we can't push the little one, we're not going to be able to move the big one," Lucía reasoned.

To her surprise, with a bit of effort, the rock rumbled slowly over the rollers and across the ground.

"There's no friction!" Lucía exclaimed.

"There is friction, just not as much," said Zac. He pointed to the first block. "See, with this block, there's all this contact between the stone and the ground. They rub against each other, making it hard to budge. That's a lot of friction."

Zac pointed next to the block on rollers. "This block isn't touching the ground at all. It only touches the rollers, and it touches them just a little. As the block moves, the rollers roll, rather than rubbing against it. That makes for a lot less friction. That's how prehistoric people can move these huge stones."

"And that's why cars and things have wheels," said Lucía.

"That's right!" said Zac. "Speaking of cars, we need to get started on our racing cart." He tapped the screen of his phone, and Stonehenge disappeared.

"You're back," said Marcus. "I guess I had that coming. What did I miss?"

"Just a little rock and roll," Ning teased.

"We learned how wheels make it easier for things to move," Lucía explained.

"Duh, I could have told you that a racing cart needs wheels!" Marcus sneered. "I mean, that's pretty basic."

"Yes, but do you understand why?" said Lucía. "The more something rubs against the ground, the more friction there is. That's what slows you down."

"Yeah, yeah, I get it," said Marcus. "Racing carts usually have pretty thin wheels. I guess big fat wheels make more friction, and that makes them slower."

"It makes sense," Lucía chimed in. "I remember my dad getting really angry one time because he was stuck driving behind a tractor. It was going super slow. And tractors have huge wheels."

"So, we'll need skinny little wheels," said Ning.

"Not so fast," said Zac. "If we make the wheels too skinny, they won't be able to handle the forces involved. They'll snap when the cart hits a bump or turns too quickly. Plus, think about race cars. Lots of race cars have wide tires, too. All that friction comes in handy when they need to grip the road, like on a turn. Without some friction, they'd slide all over the place."

"But the bigger the wheel, the heavier it is," Marcus said.

"Now, that is true," said Zac, "and the heavier something is, the more effort is needed to move it, so we need something in between."

"That's too bad. I like the idea of our cart looking like a monster truck with huge wheels," Marcus sighed. "Now that would be cool."

"Yeah, it would," laughed Zac, "but the air resistance would be terrible!"

"The what, now?" said Marcus.

"Let me guess, another force," said Lucía.

"All these forces are making my head hurt," complained Ning.

"Well, air resistance can be a headache," chuckled Zac. "When something moves, the air can push against it, slowing it down. This push is called air resistance, or drag."

"It sounds like a drag," joked Marcus.

"It is!" said Zac. "To avoid drag, our cart must be built in a shape that allows air to flow over it as easily as possible. The way air flows around something is part of a science called aerodynamics."

Zac reached into his tool box and pulled out a piece of chalk. He started drawing on the sidewalk. "A boxy shape isn't very aerodynamic." Zac drew a square on the sidewalk, with arrows to show the air passing over it. "The air pushes hard against this flat front surface, and it cannot flow smoothly around all these corners."

Next to the square, Zac drew another shape like a teardrop. The air was flowing from its rounded end. "A shape like this is a lot more aerodynamic. This rounded front splits the air, which flows smoothly over these curves."

"So, could we make the cart in a teardrop shape?" asked Lucía.

"Maybe, if we build the frame right. We could bend some thin plywood around it to form the body. It would be pretty light, too," said Zac.

"Great, then let's get started!" said Ning excitedly.

"Just one more thing before we start," said Zac. "We need to think about how we're going to power the cart."

"Will this involve your Backspace app again?" asked Marcus.

"Yeah, probably," Zac replied. "It'll be more fun than just listening to me talk."

"In that case, I'm keeping out of Lucía's way!" Marcus said. He gathered in for the photo, careful to keep Zac, Ning, and even Orbit between them. "I don't want to miss another adventure!"

Chapter 4

The Wright Idea

The virtual world appeared, and the children stood blinking in bright sunlight. A gust of wind blew up a small cloud of sand, which swirled around them.

"Oh nice!" said Marcus, coughing and spitting out sand. "Nice place you brought us to, Zac!"

"I always said you should keep your mouth closed more often, Marcus," Ning giggled.

"Is that the ocean in the distance?" asked Lucía. She shaded her eyes with her hand. "Have you brought us to the beach, Zac? I mean, it's nice and all, but it's hardly a tropical paradise."

"We're in the eastern United States," Zac announced. "This is Kill Devil Hills, near Kitty Hawk, in North Carolina. The date is December 17, 1903."

"Kill Devil Hills? Sounds friendly," said Marcus.

"Wait a minute, *Kitty Hawk* sounds familiar...."

"I thought we could learn something useful here for our racing cart," Zac said.

"They race carts here?" asked Ning, straining her eyes to see.

Suddenly, Orbit barked loudly.

"Look out!" came a cry from behind them.

The air was filled with the deafening roar of an old gasoline engine. The children spun around in time to see a machine barreling toward them through the air. It was made of wood and canvas and had two pairs of wings. A man wearing goggles was lying on one wing, struggling to control the plane by tugging on ropes. The machine twitched and jerked through the air, just above the ground.

"Duck!" shouted Zac.

The friends threw themselves to the ground as the plane swooped overhead. It blocked out the sun for a moment. Then it was gone, leaving behind the smell of gasoline and a swirl of dust.

"Sorry!" shouted another man as he ran past. He followed the plane as it skidded to a landing a short way up the beach. Zac and his friends stood up and dusted themselves off.

"I've got news for you, Zac," said Marcus. "I'm pretty sure that isn't a racing cart."

"Zac! You could have gotten us killed!" scolded Lucía.

Zac laughed. "No, no, no, we weren't in any real danger. The Backspace app just shows us a vision of history, not the real thing. It's like what really happened, but the difference is we can actually interact with it. It's… I know! Imagine you could actually crawl inside a history book and see and touch and smell everything! Yes, that's it! That's what the app does. What's happening to us right now isn't real. We're not time travelers or anything. It's like we're playing a game."

"You know, I've always wondered how that thing works," said Ning.

"Well, it felt pretty real to me," Lucía scowled.

"No, I see Zac's point," said Marcus. "I mean, I didn't even scrape my hands diving for cover." He inspected them once more, just to be sure. "Nope, not a scratch."

"Cheer up, Lucía," said Zac. "Look, the Wright brothers are coming over to talk to us."

"The Wright brothers!" Marcus exclaimed. "I knew I'd heard the name *Kitty Hawk* before! This is where the Wright brothers tested their plane. That means that the thing that almost mowed us down is the first successful airplane, the *Flyer!*"

"Marcus! I'm impressed," said Zac nodding.

"I know. It's not really fair to be this good-looking and smart, too," said Marcus.

"You are such a clown," said Ning, rolling her eyes.

"Shhh, here they come," said Zac as the two men came closer. Orbit trotted over and gave them a careful sniff.

The brothers were dressed in heavy wool suits and ties. One was balding and looked grumpy. The other had a thick mustache and a friendly smile. It was he that spoke first.

"Sorry again for the near miss. You seemed to pop up out of nowhere! Let me introduce myself.

I'm Orville Wright."

"This is my younger brother, Wilbur," he continued. "Wilbur was piloting today. He's grouchy because he hoped to take our *Flyer* even farther. Wilbur, you need to cheer up. It was our longest flight yet!" He patted his brother firmly on the back.

"I'm just sure we can make the *Flyer* go farther," muttered Wilbur. He did smile at the news that they had broken their own record.

"I'm sure you will," said Zac. "Someday, people will be able to fly from one side of the world to the other!"

The brothers stared at each other puzzled. Then they busted out laughing.

"My boy, we'll be lucky to get to the end of the beach! What an idea! Next you're going to tell us that people can fly to the moon, too!" laughed Wilbur. "Now, what can we do for you? No one comes out this way by accident, so you must be here for a reason."

"I was wondering the same thing," Lucía whispered to Ning. "This is all pretty cool, but what's their plane got to do with cart racing?"

"Actually, I was wondering if you could show us your workshop?" said Zac.

"The bicycle shop in Dayton, Ohio?" said Orville, looking puzzled. "I would've bet you wanted to talk about the *Flyer!*"

"Maybe another time, if that's okay. Right now, it's your bikes we're interested in," said Zac apologetically.

"Sure, no problem, young fellow. Do you know the way?"

"You bet," said Zac taking the cell phone from his pocket.

The friends were there literally in a flash. The beach was replaced by a workshop crammed with tools and with bikes in various stages of construction. There were tools and gears and pieces of chain everywhere.

"This looks a little like your garage, Zac," said Marcus.

"Wow, the Wright brothers build bicycles?" said Ning, taking in her surroundings.

"Yes, we do," said Orville. He appeared in the doorway, wiping his oily hands with a rag. "And not just any old bikes. I like to think we make the best bicycles in the state. Now, what is it you'd like to know?"

"Can you explain how pushing the pedals moves a bike?" asked Zac.

"Yes, of course, it's very simple. Bicycles are really very efficient machines. They are excellent at turning energy into movement. It's all because of these spiky

Sprocket

Chainring

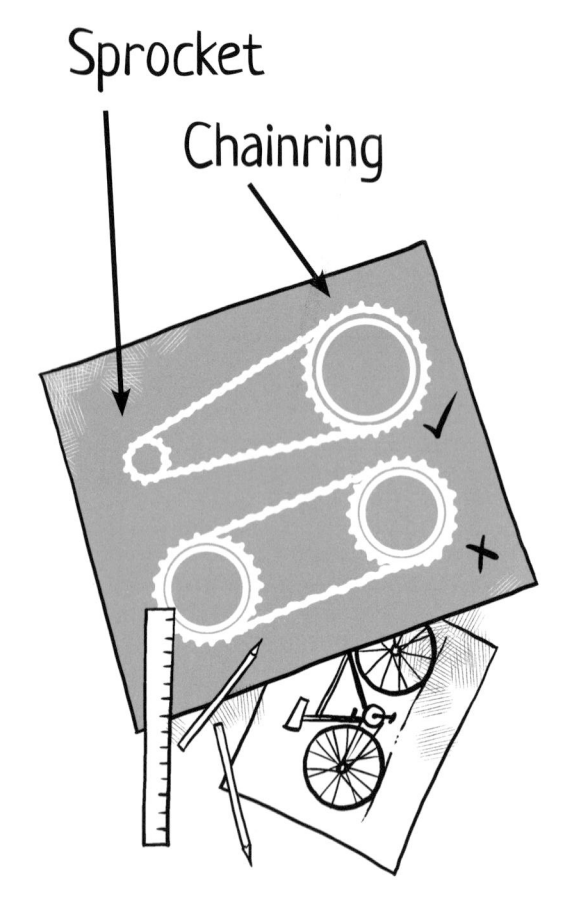

little wheels—the gears—that the chain is looped around," Orville explained.

He pointed out the parts on a bicycle propped against a workbench. "You see this big gear, attached to the pedals? We call that the chainring. The smaller one, attached to the back wheel, is the sprocket. As you can see, they are linked by a chain. Importantly, the chainring is bigger than the sprocket."

"For each complete turn of the pedals, the chainring also turns once. But because the sprocket at the back is smaller, it has to turn more times to keep up. The back wheel moves with it. So, if you turn the pedals once, the back wheel turns more than once."

"And, the bigger the chainring, and the smaller the sprocket, the faster the wheel turns," said Zac.

"Exactly, but there's a catch. It takes a lot of power to turn the back wheel so fast. So, the bigger the chainring, and the smaller the sprocket, the harder it is to pedal," added Orville. "Anyhow, why do you want to know about all this?"

"We're building a racing cart, and we're trying to figure out how to power it," Lucía replied.

"A racing cart?" said Orville, clearly unfamiliar with the idea.

"It's bit like a bicycle, but with four wheels," Lucía explained.

"Ah, I see. A quadricycle! Well, a standard chainring and sprocket set-up would give you a good balance between effort and speed," said Orville.

"Thanks again, Mr. Wright," said Zac. "If you'll excuse us, we've got a cart to build."

With a tap and a flash, the friends were back in Zac's front yard.

Chapter 5

Faster, Higher, Stronger

    Back in Zac's driveway, the children got to work building their cart. They knew that they had little time, and this seemed to help them concentrate. Zac's mom helped them saw some boards. Lucía screwed the boards together to make the frame. Marcus and Ning stripped parts from the old bicycles and an ancient baby carriage they found in the garage. They used all of this to put together the wheels, axles, and pedal system.

Zac found some thin plywood panels in the garage for the cart's body. It was finally starting to look like a racer. The children had worked hard, and everyone needed a break. Zac grabbed some bottles of water from the refrigerator, and they all took deep swigs.

Marcus pointed to the chainring. "I know Mr. Wright said this would be good enough, but I wish we had more power," he said.

"Did you have something in mind?" asked Zac, wiping his mouth with the back of his hand.

"Oh, I don't know… Ooh, yes, I do—rocket power!" Marcus exclaimed. "Imagine having a great big rocket strapped to the back!" He dashed down the driveway making whooshing noises. Orbit chased after, barking happily. "We wouldn't just win—we'd break the land speed record!"

Zac laughed. "Well, as long as we're taking a break, we might as well go and see something cool."

"Does this have anything to do with rockets?" asked

Lucía.

"You know me so well," smiled Zac.

The group huddled together, but Zac pushed away.

"One second," he said. He grabbed a tennis ball and threw it toward the open garage. Orbit chased after it. "Okay, let's do this quick before Orbit gets back. Where we're going, it's going to be way too loud for him."

Zac tapped the screen of his phone.

FLASH!

ZUMMMMMMmmmmmmm...

In the distance stood a tall metal tower, with some of its supports showing. It looked like the insides of a skyscraper halfway built. Alongside the tower stood a huge white rocket. Steam trailed in thin clouds from its sides.

"Now that's what I call a rocket!" said Ning.

"And not just any rocket," Zac replied. "That's a Saturn 5, the biggest and most powerful rocket ever built. The year is 1969. This is the Apollo 11 mission. That's the one that carried the first human beings ever to set foot on the moon. By my calculations, it should be just about to …."

Zac was drowned out by a deafening rumble that shook the ground they stood on. Great plumes of smoke billowed from the base of the rocket, hiding much of it from sight. The supports that held the rocket to the tower fell away. With a final shudder, the giant rocket surged upward.

At first, the rocket moved surprisingly slowly. But gradually, it sped up. It curved gracefully into the air, climbing higher and higher. Soon, all that could be seen was a bright point of light from its engines. A thin trail of exhaust marked its path through the sky. The friends watched in silent wonder until the light had disappeared from view.

"We… need… a… rocket… powered… cart!" shouted Marcus, breaking the silence.

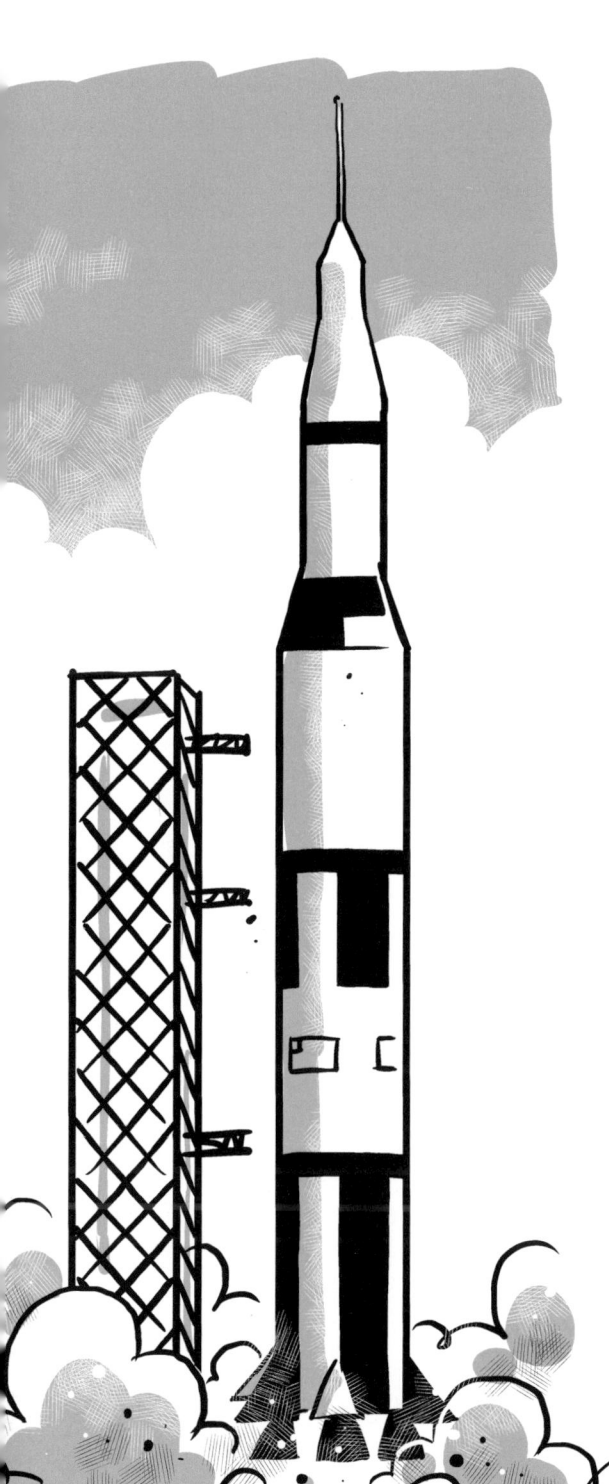

"For once, I think Marcus is right," said Ning. She slowly nodded her head, still looking up where the rocket had been.

"Oh, get real," said Lucía. "How are we going to do that? It's not like Zac's a rocket scientist!"

"Actually, the science is quite simple," said Zac. "But rather than listen to me, why not visit a real expert?" He held up the phone.

"Got anyone in mind?" asked Lucía with a smile.

"I was thinking, perhaps…" Zac tapped

the screen with his thumb.

FLASH!

ZUMMMMMMmmmmmmm...

"... Dr. Robert H. Goddard," Zac announced.

"Did someone call?" asked a man with a bushy mustache. He stood over a laboratory workbench examining what looked like a rocket engine. The device was much smaller than the huge rocket they had seen moments earlier. There was no way that the thing on the bench was going to reach outer space, but it was definitely a rocket.

"Hi, Dr. Goddard. I wondered if you might be able to explain to us how rockets work?" said Zac.

"Of course, grab a seat. You've come to the right place."

The friends perched themselves on the tall stools that stood next to the workbench. Zac whispered to the others, "Dr. Goddard did pioneering experiments in rocketry during the early 1900's."

"Rockets are a bit complicated to make, but they are surprisingly simple in theory," Goddard began. "Basically, what happens inside my rocket is that fuel is combined with oxygen, causing a chemical reaction. This is a form of combustion," he paused, in thought. "You might call it *burning*."

Goddard sketched out a rocket on a nearby chalkboard. "The combustion produces exhaust gases, which are forced out of the rocket here." He tapped his chalk at the rocket's base. "This pushes the rocket in the opposite direction."

"It's a little like when you blow up a balloon and then let it go." Goddard produced a balloon from his pocket and blew it up in three great puffs. He let go, and it darted around the room, making a funny noise. "The air shoots out one end of the balloon, and the balloon is pushed in the opposite direction. If you've heard of Sir Isaac Newton...."

"The crazy apple guy and his laws?" said Marcus.

"Ha, yes, him! Sounds like you know your science history!" said Dr. Goddard.

"We're getting there," said Lucía.

"In that case, you might understand about equal and opposite reactions. If an object pushes in one direction, the object itself will be pushed in the other. It's one of Newton's laws," the scientist explained. "Do you see?"

Zac nodded, but he wasn't so sure about the other children.

"Thank you, Dr. Goddard," he said, "but we really shouldn't take up any more of your time."

"Yeah, thanks, Doc," said Marcus, "but we need to start building our own rocket. We've got a race to win!"

Dr. Goddard said farewell, and Zac tapped the screen of his phone.

Chapter 6

A Little Leverage

Orbit bounded over to the children as soon as the Backspace app closed.

"Yeah, sorry about that," said Zac, "but you wouldn't have liked it where we were, Orbit. You don't even like the noise from the fireworks on the Fourth of July. This was like that, but much, much worse."

Orbit whined and crouched as if fireworks were about to go off. When nothing happened, he barked and jumped playfully around the children.

"Oh, Orbit, we're kind of busy," said Lucía. "Go find something to play with, boy."

"We've got to get that rocket figured out," said Marcus, looking at the cart's frame and wondering how it could be attached. "It'll be our secret weapon."

"I'm not sure that's going to work, Marcus," said Zac. "I mean, how would we steer something like that? Where would we get the fuel? Is it even safe? I don't think any of our parents would be cool with us driving around in a rocket-powered cart that we built ourselves."

"Well, that's certainly the logical answer," said Lucía.

"Don't let logic get in the way, Zac," Marcus protested. "Logic might have told the Wright brothers to stick to building bicycles. Logic might have told Sir Isaac not to sit under apple trees. Logic is boring!"

"The progress of science is guided logic, as well as imagination," Zac snapped back. "Logic may not always be exciting, but it is necessary."

"Calm down, you two," Lucía interrupted. "I can settle this rocket thing once and for all. The rules say no engines." She showed them the flier that Marcus had found. "And, a rocket is a kind of engine."

"Well, that settles it," said Ning. She pushed away Orbit, who was jumping all over her. Zac and Marcus went back to working on the cart in silence.

"What's wrong, Orbit? Are you bored? Do you want to play?" said Ning. Orbit ran to the tree and started barking up at the branches. "Oh, the Frisbee!" Ning started to feel guilty again. "Sorry, Orbit, but it's stuck."

"What's wrong?" asked Marcus.

"Before you got here, Ning threw Orbit's Frisbee into the tree," said Lucía.

"It was an accident!" Ning protested. "I keep telling you, the wind took it."

Marcus stood at the foot of the tree and looked up. "It's pretty high up there. You could try throwing something up to knock it down. But even if you could, you might just get something else stuck up there."

"How about we stand on one another's shoulders, like a human pyramid or something?" said Ning.

"That still wouldn't be high enough, and I doubt we'd be strong enough anyway," Lucía replied. "Any ideas, Zac?"

"If we could somehow lift one of us into the tree … hmmmm …." said Zac, scratching his head as he thought. "Okay, I don't know, but I know someone who might." He pulled the cell phone from his pocket, and the rest of the children gathered around.

FLASH!

ZUMMMMMMmmmmmmm…

"Ooh, this is nice and warm," said Lucía. She took a step, and dust rose from the packed earth beneath her feet.

The children were standing in a small, open square surrounded by walls of whitewashed brick. It was the courtyard of a large house. The house was two stories tall, with a wooden balcony that ran around the second floor. The balcony was shaded by the roof, which was covered in red clay tiles. The windows were small and set high in the walls, and they did not have any glass in them. The children heard someone call out.

A man waved to them from the balcony. He had a big gray beard and was dressed in loose clothing. He spoke again and then disappeared inside the house.

"I didn't understand a word of that," said Ning.

"That's because he was ancient Greek," said Zac.

"Well, that guy looked old, but I wouldn't call him ancient," said Marcus.

Zac was not sure if Marcus was kidding. "No, I mean he is from ancient Greece. The date is 225 B.C. The guy we just saw was Archimedes, one of the greatest scientists from early history."

"He sounds great, but there's not much point in visiting him if we can't understand what he's saying," said Lucía.

"Don't worry," said Zac, "the Backspace app has a translate function. I'll turn it on now."

Archimedes appeared in a doorway and stepped into the courtyard.

"Hello, my friends," he said. He smiled as he walked toward them. "My apologies for the delay. I'm not getting any younger, and I swear they keep adding more stairs each time I have to climb them! Now, what brings you here?"

"We need to get into a tree that is too tall to climb. We were thinking of lifting one of us up into it, but we're not strong enough. Besides, it's too high for us to reach like that anyway. I wondered if you had an invention that could help," said Zac.

Archimedes laughed, "You want to get into a tree?" He shrugged, then drew with his finger in the dusty courtyard. He traced a small triangle with a long line over the top. It looked a little bit like a lopsided seesaw. On the short end, he drew a box and on the long end, an arrow pointing down.

"Give me a long enough lever, and I shall move the whole world," said Archimedes. He patted Zac on the back, then shuffled back indoors.

Zac slapped himself on the forehead. "Of course," he said.

"That's it?" said Lucía in disbelief. "We came to ancient Greece for a dusty drawing of a seesaw?"

"That's all we need," said Zac. "And it's not a seesaw, it's a lever, like Archimedes said." Zac pointed to the triangle. "This is called the *fulcrum,* or pivot. The lever is like a board that rests on top of it. You put the thing you want to lift on the short end of the lever," Zac said, pointing to the box. "Then you push down on the long end. It's really simple, but it works really well."

"The longer the end you push on is, the easier it is to lift the load. If that end is four times longer than the end with the load on it, for example, you only need a quarter of the effort to lift the object. With a long enough lever, we'd be strong enough to lift one of us into the tree."

"That must be how those people at Stonehenge got those huge stone blocks onto the rollers. I'd been wondering about that!" said Lucía.

"Maybe!" said Zac. "People have used levers to move things for thousands of years, and we still do it today!"

"Well then, what are we waiting for?" said Marcus. "Let's get leave-r-ing! Get it? Honestly, my comic genius is wasted on all of you!"

Chapter 7
Under Pressure

Back in Zac's driveway, the children were excited about the lever for exactly 3.5 seconds. That's how long it took them to spot the flaw in their plan.

"How big a lever are we going to need to lift one of us into a tree?" Lucía asked. "I mean, do we even have enough wood to make something that big?"

"It's not just the lever—it's the fulcrum that the lever sits on, too. That would have to be at least half as tall as the tree," Zac added. "No, a lever isn't going to work. It looks like we'll just have to wait for gravity and a strong wind to bring the Frisbee down for us."

"Now, if I had rockets in my shoes, I could fly up there like Iron Man," said Marcus. Orbit looked at him expectantly. "Sorry, boy, but I don't have rocket shoes. It was just a stupid idea." Marcus picked up one of the plastic water bottles that Zac had brought out earlier and took a swig.

"Maybe it's not that stupid," said Lucía. "Zac, if a balloon can fly around just by letting out air, could a small rocket do the same thing?"

Zac scratched the back of his head, deep in thought. He looked over at the old bicycles he'd been working on. Inspiration struck. "That's it! Yes, that should work! Marcus, I'll need that water bottle, please. In fact, I'm going to need all your water bottles. Lucía and Marcus, could you check the recycling bin to see if you can find any more? Ning, would you get the basketball pump from the garage, please? I'll need to go and grab some things from my shelves."

Moments later, Zac was back with some small corks and several pairs of safety goggles. Lucía and Marcus returned with their arms full of plastic bottles of various sizes. Ning came back with a handheld ball pump. "Is this what you wanted?" she asked.

"That's the one. Now, could you all please put on these safety goggles. Marcus, can I have your bottle? Thank you. Great, it looks about a quarter full. That's perfect."

Zac removed the cap and pushed a cork into the mouth of the bottle. "Now, what I'm going to do is pump air into the bottle." He carefully pushed the pump's needle into the cork until the tip came out inside the bottle. Then, he began to work the plunger, pumping air into the bottle. "Okay, everybody, stand back! Any minute, the pressure is going to build up so much it will push the cork out of the bottle."

Zac kept pumping. With a sudden pop, the bottle shot away, showering them all with water. It zoomed across the front yard, spraying water the whole way. The makeshift rocket finally bounced off the tree trunk and landed on the lawn. Orbit chased happily after it. He fetched the bottle back to Zac.

"That was AMAZING!" shouted Marcus, jumping around. "My turn next!"

"It's not very accurate, but, yeah, it's pretty cool," Zac admitted.

"Let's get a bit closer to the tree," Lucía suggested.

"That might make it easier to hit the Frisbee."

For the next 10 minutes, they took turns shooting rockets at the tree. Zac was right—the rockets were not accurate. But, they were fun, and Orbit enjoyed chasing each one that missed the target. As Ning loaded up another bottle, Zac explained how the rockets worked.

"It's all about the water," said Zac. "Remember what Dr. Goddard said about Newton's laws? Every action has an equal and opposite reaction. The water comes shooting out the mouth of the bottle. That pushes the bottle in the opposite direction."

"But why do we have to put water in the bottles?" asked Ning. "Couldn't we just use air?"

"That has to do with another of Newton's laws," Zac explained. "It says that the effect of a force on an object depends on the object's mass—basically how heavy it is," Zac explained. "Imagine pushing a wagon. An empty wagon is nice and light, so you can probably push it pretty fast. Now imagine that the wagon is full of heavy rocks. You'd have to push pretty hard to get it moving even a little. In both cases, your push provides the same amount of force. But it takes more effort to get the heavy wagon moving."

"What does that have to do with the rocket?" said Ning, puzzled.

"We put water in the rocket because water is heavier than air," Zac continued. "It takes more force to push it out of the bottle. But remember, that force has an equal and opposite reaction. It pushes the bottle the other way. The bottle is much lighter than the water. The same amount of force causes the lightweight bottle to zoom off."

"So, Apple Guy gave us bottle rockets!" said Marcus, wiping water off his face. "He's getting cooler all the time!"

"We don't have many bottles left," interrupted Ning.

"No problem," said Lucía, lining up her next shot. "I've got a good feeling about this one."

She pumped until the bottle shot away. It sailed up into the branches, striking a direct hit on the Frisbee. The dislodged Frisbee tumbled toward the ground. Delighted, Orbit snatched it up mid-air.

The friends high-fived one another and congratulated Lucía on her rocketry skills.

"One problem," said Ning nodding toward the tree. "How do we get all those down?"

The children looked up at the tree. Dozens of plastic water bottles were now lodged in its branches. It looked like some kind of weird art exhibit, or a Christmas tree decorated with trash.

"I think we'll wait for wind and gravity this time," said Zac. "In the meantime, I hope my parents don't look up there. I'm not sure I want to explain this."

Chapter 8
Look Out Below!

It took a couple more hours, but the racing cart was nearly complete. Lucía screwed the last pieces of plywood to the cart's frame. Marcus made sure that the chainring and sprocket were connected properly. Ning tested the system of ropes that Zac had fitted for steering. Zac himself studied the race route on a large paper map that he had spread out on the lawn.

"I just realized something," said Lucía, putting down her screwdriver. "We haven't decided who's driving yet."

"I'm smallest and lightest," said Ning, "and I really like speed, so it should be me."

"Hold on a minute," said Marcus. "Surely it depends on the route. I bet it's mainly downhill. In that case, I think we should pick the heaviest driver. That will make the cart go faster. What do you think, Zac?"

"Well, you're right about the route," said Zac, tracing

it on the map with his finger. "But, I'm not sure whether you'd be faster or not."

"I bet you know of someone you can ask, though," said Lucía. The group was already gathering into a huddle.

"I bet I do," said Zac, pulling out his cell phone.

FLASH!

ZUMMMMMMmmmmmmm...

The scene around them transformed from Zac's yard into a town square. Zac and his friends were standing on an open plaza paved with brown stones. People dressed in dark clothing wandered about, talking or carrying their shopping in baskets. Behind the children rose the bell tower of a church.

"We're not at the mall," said Lucía, "Not unless fashion has taken a turn for the worse."

"No, we're in a place called Holland, in Europe, in 1586—in the town of Delft, to be precise," said Zac.

"Oh, and I'd take a step back now, if I were you," Zac cautioned. Suddenly, two large metal balls thudded to the ground in front of them. They landed at the same time, ringing out a single, low clang.

"Do you remember when you said we were totally safe in the Backspace app?" said Lucía slowly. She was trying her best to stay calm. "What would happen if one of those balls had hit us?"

"You know, I'm not sure," said Zac. "Probably nothing."

"Your use of the word *probably* doesn't fill me with confidence," added Lucía.

The group examined the two lead balls that had come to rest on the pavement. One was the size of a softball. The other was bigger than a basketball. They both looked very heavy. Suddenly, a man appeared at the children's side. He was dressed in dark clothing like the rest. Zac switched on the Backspace app's translation feature.

"Did they hit the ground at the same time?" the man asked.

The friends nodded.

"Yes! You see, it's correct! Two objects of different mass will fall at the same speed. I have proved it!"

"*Mass* is the scientific word for how much matter is in something," Zac explained to his puzzled friends. "It's similar to weight, but it's not exactly the same thing."

"That's Simon Stevin, by the way." Zac pointed to the man. "He just dropped those two balls from that church tower. He's testing an idea made famous by another scientist, an Italian named Galileo. Galileo thought that, all things being equal, objects dropped at the same time would fall at the same rate, even if one had more mass than the other. But why am I explaining this? Let's talk to Galileo himself."

Zac tapped the screen on his phone. In an instant, they flashed from Holland to Italy.

The busy town square was replaced by a quiet, airy room. A bearded man stood next to a wooden ramp. The ramp had a groove lined with metal running down its middle. Nearby, water dripped steadily from a large metal cone into a bucket. The man took a metal ball and placed it in the groove. As the ball rolled down the ramp, he counted the *plunk! plunk! plunk!* of the water drops as they fell into the bucket. The room was very quiet. The children hear the pen scratch as he wrote down his observations.

"What's going on?" whispered Lucía.

"That's Galileo," answered Zac, "one of the most important scientists in history. He was a total genius. At the moment, he's doing an experiment to determine how fast objects fall under the pull of gravity."

"Just like Simon Stevin!" Lucía whispered.

"Most people at the time believed the ancient Greek scientist Aristotle," Zac continued. "Aristotle thought that if two objects were dropped from the same height, the heavier one would fall faster."

"But I can prove he's wrong!" boomed Galileo, the sudden noise making them jump. "I thank you for your courtesy in staying quiet while I worked. You have a respect for science in action. I admire that in people so young. Come, have a look."

He waved some papers at them and pointed at the ramp. "See here, if we simply drop two balls of different mass, they will fall too fast for us to accurately judge their speed. So, I've built this ramp." The friends nodded.

"The slope draws out their fall, so I can time their motion using my water clock here." Galileo pointed at the dripping cone.

"The steady drip of water is like the ticking of a clock," Zac observed.

"When I roll balls of different mass, they seem to move at the same speed. Aristotle was wrong!"

"Nice work, Mr. G.," said Marcus, "I mean, Galileo, sir!"

"Thank you for your time," said Zac.

"You young people are always welcome, always welcome," said Galileo with a wave. "It's a pleasure to talk to those who wish to learn."

The room disappeared from view, and Zac's front yard reappeared.

"Well, it's settled then—I'll drive," said Ning. "Galileo pretty much said so. And, Zac said Galileo is a genius. Who's going to argue with a genius?"

"Wait just a minute," said Zac. "If mass were the only factor, you'd both roll downhill at the same speed. But there's friction and wind resistance to consider. It's a lot more complicated than dropping metal balls."

Ning looked crushed. Marcus beamed at Zac expectantly.

"Not only that, but the course is not all downhill." Zac showed them the map. The first and final sections of the race were uphill. The last leg in particular was a long, gentle rise to the finish line. "On the whole, I think that Ning would be a better driver on this course, with her light weight and her daring." Ning pumped her fist in triumph.

"Yeah, okay," Marcus shrugged. "I trust your decision, even if you're not as big a genius as Mr. G. Just make sure you win, Ning, or I'll make sure you never forget it."

"Aw, thanks, Marcus," said Ning, "and don't worry. I'll win!"

"That's not all we should thank Marcus for," said Zac, suddenly grinning from ear to ear. "All his talk about a secret weapon has given me an idea!"

Chapter 9
The Secret Weapon

The next day, the weather was clear and dry, but it was still windy. The friends gathered at Zac's house, ready for the big race. They had worked late into the night to finish building the cart. So Marcus, Ning, and Lucía were surprised to find that something new had been added.

"Why is there a big pole sticking up at the front of the cart?" asked Lucía.

"That's our secret weapon!" said Zac proudly.

"So what is it, then?" asked Marcus. "It looks more like a stick than a secret weapon. Is it like a lance for Ning to poke the other carts out of the way?"

"I'd tell you, but I don't want to ruin the surprise," said Zac. "I can say that it's not a lance. Ning, I'd better tell you, though, so you know what to do."

Zac took Ning aside and let her in on the secret. Lucía and Marcus shrugged at each other as they watched the other two whispering together. At first, Ning looked puzzled. Zac was explaining something using a lot of hand gestures. Suddenly, Ning broke into a broad smile, and she nodded with excitement.

"Okay, let's get going," said Zac, clapping his hands together.

"The surprise certainly seems to have you excited, Ning," said Lucía.

"Yeah! It's genius, believe me," Ning replied.

"Come on, we don't have time to talk about how brilliant I am, the race starts soon!" said Zac.

As the children approached the starting area, it was clear that the race had attracted plenty of attention.

The starting area was crowded with racing carts of various shapes and sizes. Some of them looked like they would fall apart at the first bump in the road. Others appeared to have been built by professionals. A big crowd had shown up to watch the race, too. The roads had been closed, and temporary seating had been set up around the course. The route was marked with bright banners that snapped in the breeze. Bales of hay on the turns served as safety barriers. Zac and his friends pushed their cart through the crowd to the starting line.

Lucía looked around, checking out the competition. "We'll need to get a good start to beat some of these carts," she whispered. "See if we can get our cart as close to the starting line as possible. We should have come earlier and grabbed a good spot!" To her surprise, however, Zac told them to push the cart farther back. The friends look puzzled as they wheeled the cart to the very back of the pack. Even then, Zac told them to keep going!

"Where are you taking us?" asked Marcus, in disbelief.

"To around … here. That should do it," said Zac, smiling proudly.

"But we're 30 lengths behind everyone else!" Lucía said. "I thought we needed a good start to have a chance at winning."

"Take a look at the course," said Zac. "The start is uphill. But where we are, back here, we get to go downhill first. Ning will be up to top speed in no time, while the rest are still huffing and puffing near the starting line."

"Okay," said Ning doubtfully, "but I don't like to lose!"

"Of course you don't," said Zac. "That's what why you're our driver!"

"Well, if it's good enough for you two, it's good enough for me," said Marcus, pushing the cart into position.

"Yeah, good luck," said Lucía, helping Ning to put on her safety helmet. "All right, they're about to start! We'll grab a seat in the bleachers. We can see most of the course from there."

Zac, Lucía, and Marcus found their seats. They were just in time to see the race official drop his flag, starting the race. The carts sprang forward. The lighter carts jumped out to an early lead. The heavier ones struggled up the gentle slope.

The friends noticed that many of the other carts were pedal-powered, like their own. The rest were scooted along by the driver's feet or pushed from behind by a team of people. One cart was even driven by pulling handheld levers. It looked complicated and quickly broke, rolling back toward the starting line.

Suddenly, Ning was there, flying past the stragglers. She pedaled furiously. Even at a distance, the friends could see her face all scrunched with effort. The course twisted through a few turns, testing the carts' steering. Many of them ran up against the hay bales that lined the route. Others knocked into one another and ground to a halt. Ning swept around the turns with ease, thanks to her sharp driving and well-built cart. She weaved in and out of the slow and stopped carts. Soon, there were only three carts in front of her.

"Go, Ning. Go!" shouted Marcus. It was a thrilling race, but Zac looked strangely distracted.

"What's wrong, Zac? You look worried." asked Lucía.

"I don't really know," Zac replied. "I have this feeling that I forgot to do something."

"Like what?" asked Marcus. "The cart is working great. Its wheels have the perfect combination of size and strength. We've got the pedals, the chainring, and the sprockets all working. And, you've attached your mysterious secret weapon."

"Yeah, it's probably nothing," said Zac, shaking his head. "I probably just forgot to do a homework assignment or something. Oh, look, Ning's caught up with another one!"

There were just two carts ahead of Ning as the race entered the long, gentle slope up to the finish line. Ning's cart was lighter than the one in second place, and she slowly overtook it. It took every last drop of effort, but she refused to give up.

"Just one cart to catch," shouted Marcus, "and Ning's gaining all the time!"

"I think the lead cart is too far ahead," said Lucía in dismay. "She won't catch it!"

Zac cupped his hands around his mouth and yelled as loud as he could, "Ning, the secret weapon! NOW!"

Ning hauled on a rope, and a broad white sail unfurled. It climbed quickly up the pole, which the Marcus and Lucía now realized was a mast. A stiff wind filled the sail. It was as if the cart had become turbo-charged. Ning shot up the slope, gaining on the lead cart faster than ever.

"Ning's going to do it!" cried Lucía.

"Oh no!" said Zac.

"What do you mean? Your secret weapon's going to win it for us!" said Marcus.

"I've just remembered what I forgot," cried Zac. "I forgot to give the cart brakes!"

Chapter 10
Give Me a Brake

Ning pedaled as hard and as fast as she could, unaware of any danger. They were almost to the finish line, but the other cart was nearly close enough to touch. Ning recognized the driver as the captain of the junior high school soccer team. He was lean and strong, but Ning could tell he was tiring. He was pedaling slower and slower.

The slowing of her rival inspired one last boost of energy in Ning. She gritted her teeth and cranked away at the pedals, just as the breeze picked up again. The cart edged ahead and flew over the finish line! She'd won!

"YES!" Ning shouted, pumping her fist in delight. The crowd cheered. Ning looked over to the bleachers to where Zac and the others were sitting. She could see them waving wildly.

"Ning," they shouted, "there's a problem!"

Ning waved back at them and smiled. She could not hear what they were saying. She was enjoying her moment of victory.

The winner's stand was up ahead, and she could see the race officials waiting. They motioned for her to slow down. She eased off the pedals, and reached for the brakes. That was when she realized that there weren't any!

"Sorry, I can't stop!" she cried. She swerved to

avoid the surprised officials, who dove out of the runaway cart's path. The wind puffed up the sail again, and the cart was moving pretty quickly. Ning couldn't turn too sharply or she would risk tipping over.

"Okay, calm down, Ning," she said to herself. "Concentrate. It's just like you're in the race again. Look for a safe route to drive."

Ning saw a stretch of road that had been closed off for the race. She headed for that.

"What would Zac tell me to do?" she wondered. "He'd tell me to use what I know about forces." She hauled on the steering ropes, narrowly missing a jogger who was wandering down the road. "So figure it out, Ning. Figure it out."

Meanwhile, Lucía, Marcus, and Zac were running down the road trying to catch up with her.

"She's going too fast!" gasped Marcus, already out of breath.

"If she could only steer it uphill, it would help," said Lucía.

"No," said Zac. "What she needs to do first is…"

"Of course!" said Ning. "If I release the sail, then the wind won't be pushing me along!" She unhooked the rope, and the sail flopped onto the hood of the cart. The cart was no longer speeding up. But it was still traveling quickly, and she had no way to slow it down. "Friction will slow me down eventually," she thought, "but how long will that take?"

She turned sharply to avoid a traffic barrier, just brushing past it. Zac, Lucía, and Marcus cut the corner, getting close enough now to shout.

"Ning, take the next right turn—it'll take you uphill and slow you down!" shouted Marcus.

"Good thinking, Marcus," said Zac. "If only there was a big pile of sand around here. That would really increase the friction and slow her down."

"But here in the real world, Zac, we're a long way from the nearest beach. The Backspace app can't solve this problem," snapped Lucía. "Come on, think of a better plan before she crashes!"

"Sorry," said Zac. "I was just hoping there might be a construction site around here or a playground with a big sandbox. I didn't think she was going to drive all the way to the beach!"

"Can you two stop arguing and do more chasing?" panted Marcus.

Ning raced toward the next turn but then—disaster! She pulled on the steering ropes, but nothing happened.

"I can't steer!" she shouted. "The sail must be tangled with the steering ropes!"

Instead of turning right, the cart continued forward, straight toward a downhill slope. It picked up speed and disappeared from sight down the hill.

The friends could no longer see Ning, but they could sure hear her.

"HHHHHHEEEEEEELLLLLLPPPPPPP!!!!!" she screamed. Her voice grew fainter and fainter as the cart carried her farther away.

Suddenly the children heard a

CRASH!

There was a brief silence, then

SPLASH!

Zac, Lucía, and Marcus looked at one another, worried.

"What's down there?" asked Marcus.

"The park," said Zac.

"With the duck pond!" said Lucía.

They sprinted down the hill. A low hedge surrounded the park. There was a fresh hole in it about the size of the racing cart. Zac, Lucía, and Marcus ducked through the hole and followed track marks across the grass. There, in the middle of the duck pond, sat Ning and the overturned cart. A family of ducks paddled by, looking surprised.

"Ah look, the water slowed her down!" said Zac. "You see, the water acted in much the same way as sand would have."

"Ning, are you okay?" shouted Lucía.

Ning nodded yes, but she had an angry glare on her face. She was completely soaked from the crash. Water dripped from her helmet.

"Ah, now, this is quite interesting," said Zac. "As the weight of the cart pushes down on the water, the water pushes up against it. The cart is actually floating. More forces at work!"

"Somehow, I don't think Ning is in the mood to hear about it," replied Lucía.

"Yes, best not force that issue," said Marcus, "or I think she'll be using some other forces—on you."

"I think the cart's starting to sink," said Lucía.

"Yes it is—water must be leaking in through the bottom," said Marcus.

"Can Ning even swim?" asked Lucía, worried.

"Oh, she'll be fine, the pond's only knee deep," said Zac. Then he saw Ning's face as she stomped through the water toward them. "Uh oh," said Zac. "She doesn't look happy, does she?"

"Nope," said Marcus.

"In fact," added Lucía, "I think she looks pretty furious."

"I wonder if she's mad at anyone in particular," said Marcus, winking at Lucía.

"Oh, I'm sure she's just embarrassed because she crashed the racing cart," said Zac.

"Zac Newton!" Ning shouted. "When I get my hands on you…"

"I don't know, but it sounds to me like she definitely thinks one of us is to blame," said Lucía.

"Ah. Yes … um … oh, I've just remembered,"

stammered Zac, "I was supposed to take Orbit for a walk. I better run and do it now. See you later!"

Marcus and Lucía laughed as Zac turned and ran. Ning, soaking wet, followed close on his heels.

Meet the Scientists

Isaac Newton

Sir Isaac Newton (1642–1727) was a British scientist and mathematician. He developed laws of motion, made discoveries about light, and invented a new kind of mathematics called calculus.

The Wright brothers

Wilbur (1867–1912) and Orville (1871–1948) Wright built the world's first successful powered flying machine. The brothers made their pioneering flight on Dec. 17, 1903, near Kitty Hawk, North Carolina.

Robert H. Goddard

Robert Hutchings Goddard (1882–1945) was a pioneer in the field of rocketry. In 1926, he invented a rocket powered by gasoline and liquid oxygen.

Archimedes

Archimedes (*ahr kuh MEE deez*) (287?–212 B.C.) was an ancient Greek inventor, mathematician, scientist, and engineer. He is thought to have invented, among other things, a device for moving water now called the Archimedean screw.

Simon Stevin

Simon Stevin (1548–1620) was a Flemish mathematician, scientist, and inventor. He is best known for developing and promoting the use of decimal fractions.

Galileo

Galileo (*gal uh LAY oh*) (1564–1642) was an Italian scientist and astronomer. In addition to his studies of movement, he made a number of discoveries about the solar system. He was the first person to observe the moons of Jupiter.

Meet the Scientists

Glossary

aerodynamics the scientific study of the motion of air around objects

air resistance the pushing back of the air against an object moving through it; also called drag

chainring the large, front gear of a bicycle. It turns with the pedals.

combustion burning

exhaust the escape of gases from an engine

flier a piece of paper printed with information; a handout

force a push or pull; anything that changes the motion of an object

fulcrum the point on which a lever turns; sometimes called a *pivot*

friction the resistance between two objects that rub against each other

gravity the force that, on Earth, tends to pull everything downward

lance a historical weapon that looks like a long spear

mass the amount of matter in something. Matter is the stuff of which all objects are made. Mass is related to weight, but it is not exactly the same thing.

mast the pole that holds a sail

pressure the force of something pressing or pushing against an object

rocket an engine that works by shooting out exhaust. The rocket is pushed in the opposite direction.

scientific law a statement that explains how something works

selfie an informal self-portrait, usually taken with a cell phone

sprocket the smaller, rear gear of a bicycle. It turns the back wheel.

virtual created and existing only in a computer—like the historical scenes visited in Zac's Backspace app

water clock a device that uses the dripping of water to measure the passing of time

Additional Resources

Books

Crash Course in Forces and Motion with Max Axiom, Super Scientist
Emily Sohn (Capstone Press, 2016)

Forces and Motion (Mind Webs)
Anna Claybourne (Wayland, 2016)

Simple Machines: Forces in Action (Do It Yourself)
Buffy Silverman (Heinemann, 2016)

Horrible Science: Fatal Forces
Nick Arnold (Scholastic, 2014)

Websites

BBC Bitesize – Forces Class Clips
http://www.bbc.co.uk/education/topics/zpxf9j6/resources/1

A series of videos demonstrating different types of force in a fun way.

Galileo Facts For Kids
https://www.coolkidfacts.com/galileo-facts-for-kids/

Meet Galileo and discover all the amazing things he worked on, from forces to astronomy.

Science Zone: Forces and Magnets
http://www.primaryhomeworkhelp.co.uk/revision/Science/physical.htm

Games, videos, and questions to test your knowledge on everything you know about forces.

Index

air resistance 27, 28, 72

Archimedes 54–57, 93

bottle rockets 59–64

chainrings 38–40

friction 19, 23–26, 85

Galileo 69–72, 93

Goddard, Robert 46–49, 92

gravity 17

laws of motion 17, 48, 62

levers 56–58

mass 62, 68–72

Newton, Sir Isaac 14–17, 92

rockets 42–49, 59–64

Saturn 5 rocket 43–45

sprockets 38–39

Stevin, Simon 68–70, 93

Stonehenge 21–25, 57

wheels 24–26, 38–39

Wright brothers 31–40